Flying In My Dreams

Ange D. Sprunger

ISBN: 979-8-9877217-0-4

DEDICATION

I dedicate this book to my daughter Kai who has an exquisite heart and mind.
Her art adds beauty to the world and, she continues authorship to the next generation.

I dedicate this book to my friend Karen who, as a child, graded the notes we exchanged and,
as an adult, assists with grammatical questions.

I dedicate this book to my friend M.B. He views my words as a gift.
He inspired me to write again after a long poetic hiatus.

I dedicate this book to my dear friend Lucy.
For almost four decades thus far, she demonstrates the true meaning of friendship.

I dedicate this book to my husband Rene. He handles the household responsibilities
when I write and provides technical support.

And finally, I dedicate this book to God.
He places people in circumstances where they can use their talents and abilities
to best fulfill their purpose.

ACKNOWLEDGEMENTS

Illustrations by Tricia Robinson Harvey:
The Eyes
Severed Heart
Synergy
Vile Love
The Pier
Imprisoned Emotions—The Final Plague
The Tree
Soul Hugs
Dry Bones Come Alive
Life

Photographs by Ange D. Sprunger:
The Cross
Flying Beyond and Within
The Puzzle
Nighttime
Vain Vows
Symphony of Waves
Time
Soar on Wings Like Eagles
A Few of My Favorite Things
Ode to the Lighthouse
In Pursuit of Naught
Dreams
Journey to the Land of the Purple Flowers
Tomorrow
Inspiration
Imperfect
Mom
Apprehending the Thieves of Lost Words
Jacob
Hurricane Ian
The Last Plight

Illustration by Alex Chen:
"Betta You Can Learn a Lesson from a Fish"

Illustration by Karen Burkwall Johnson:
What the Fox Squirrel Didn't Say

Digital illustration by Kai Sprunger:
The Face
Hairline Fractures in the Heart

Illustrations by Anonymous:
"Do Not Give Up"
Lost Chances
Shadow Dance (Valedictory)

Illustrations by Rene Sprunger:
Destination—Freedom
The Collection

For the poem *Jacob*, a google.com search of the name "Jacob" said that it meant "supplanter." Synonyms for "supplanter" were listed in www.wordhippo.com and www.thesaurus.com. A dozen synonyms that appeared in both lists were included in my poem *Jacob*.

Words from the Holy Bible, Ezekiel 37:1-10 New International Version, were referenced in the poem *Dry Bones Come Alive*. This was from www.biblegateway.com > NIV.

The photo for the poem *Time* is a picture of the author's mother holding a Fisher Price Clock that was owned by her or by the author for more than fifty years.

The poem, *What the Fox Squirrel Didn't Say*, included references to *The Lorax* (Dr. Seuss Enterprises, L.P., 1971.) and *Horton Hears a Who* (Dr. Seuss Enterprises, L.P., 1954; 1982.) Theodor Seuss Geisel—aka Dr. Seuss—is the author of these books.

Words from the Holy Bible, John 21:18 New International Version, were quoted in the poem *Imperfect*. This was from www.bible.com > NIV.

The photo of the word "*Love*" for the poem, *The Cross*, was of sand art produced by Kai Sprunger.

Three poems: "*Do Not Give Up*", *Lost Chances*, and *Shadow Dance* (*Valedictory*) included illustrations by an artist who wishes to remain anonymous. This was work for hire.

TABLE OF CONTENTS

Introduction

Between the past and the future

there lies a small gap of time—

seize it quickly before it vanishes.

The Eyes
(Written at age 16)

There you are, quietly sitting beside me,
and all I can think of are your eyes.
They glare gently towards those who pass by,
and entice potential lovers,
to plunge into their green ocean.

The waves are rising high.
I am drowning!
Where are you?
I am spinning in a deep sea of colors.
Love is engulfing my being.
I can't see!
I no longer exist.
I have been swallowed by your eyes.

Only when I look away,
am I released from their grasp.
Even then, their twinkle remains
implanted in my mind.

One glance
is a spark of life,
to an empty heart.
I yearn to embrace you,
and to look freely into your emerald abyss.
If only a voice
could accompany their smiling silence,
and blossom into a friendship.

January 15, 1982

The Cross
(Written at age 16)

When I look at the grace of the cross,
all I see is love.

I feel the presence of Your Spirit;
I know You are there.

I understand your scriptures;
You make Your words clear.

When I silently pray to You,
my faith becomes a shield.

Your love remains forever;
I feel Your power.

When I hold Your cross in my hand,
I'm reminded that You care.

You guide me on all my paths;
You remove my doubt and fear.

I can do what is best for all my days,
If I choose to follow You.

I can reach beyond my limitations,
If it is done for You.

The greatest change Your cross has made
as it shined on my life,
is the heart of love You have given to me
when You chose to give Your life.

February 22, 1982

Flying Beyond and Within
(Written at age 17)

Trust in me as I have trusted in you.
Together we can soar beyond and within.
Don't get lost in the darkness.
Walk beside me in the light.

Grow into you and allow me to grow into me.
Together we can touch life's wonders
and accomplish what we can't achieve alone.

Pray for me while I pray for you.
Even when we are apart,
our thoughts will still be united.

Smile for me when I can no longer smile.
When I can't hold myself up,
let me lean on you.

I will reach for you when you can't reach me.
I will speak for you when you have lost your words.

Let's believe in each other
and live as connected parts of a whole.
As we fly towards heaven,
we can fly within.

Love me forever as I plan to love you.

January 27, 1983

"Do Not Give Up"
(Written at age 17)

You are there beside me,
helping me along the way.
Sometimes it takes the support of a friend,
to guide and lend a hand.
You are here as I.
Together we run the same race.
You also struggle to finish.
Together we move on.
The strength of one becomes the power of the other.
The weaknesses of one are overcome
by the soft pleas of the other.
You tell me to finish.
I feel energy.
Together we complete the race.
Together we have finished.
The one who was my opponent
has helped me as a friend.
I thank you for saying to me, "Do not give up."
These words remain in my mind.
I repeat them to other strangers
who have fallen behind.
I whisper softly as one had whispered to me,
"Do not give up."
Together we will help one another.
Just as in this race,
we will run together.
The path of life is filled with struggles
but it also has much beauty.
You are still beside me.
Together we will move on.
Together we will finish.
Do not give up.

March 9, 1983

The Puzzle

A relationship is a puzzle of life.
Its pieces are glued over time.
Each piece is unique.
Some fit together; some don't.
No two pieces can be placed simultaneously.

In relationship puzzles,
the final picture is obscured
just as one's destiny is veiled
and only occasionally revealed.
Hope strengthens even the weakest image.

I sort through the different pieces
of my relationships
just as one might rummage through
the different pieces of a puzzle
to find the border pieces.
Suddenly, I'm faced with a war between my emotions.
I'm confused how I feel,
and I don't want to fight.

As I prepare to battle my feelings,
in vain, I try to disguise the cry of love
and squelch its fury with angry daggers.
Alas, the daggers are owned by Cupid.

I have unleashed the leech-like hold of jealousy
with a kiss.
Who can contend against love
when the foe is within the soul?

Unlike a house of blocks which can be knocked down
by a child who doesn't love it,
the vigor of two beating hearts
is torn apart by none.
Seize young love.

April 8, 1986

AC
4/15/21.

"Betta You Can Learn a Lesson from a Fish"

Fins of indigo and magenta flare vigorously
at the magnified mirror image on the tiny tank wall.
Frantically leaping at a fictitious and hateful foe,
the foolish Betta,
alias Siamese Fighting Fish,
senselessly (yet unknowingly) battles himself.

Flaunting its supposed dominance
to tease the threatening mirage,
the confident enraged assailant protects his territory
by lunging fiercely against the glass.
As would be expected,
its opponent attacks simultaneously
in a path directly opposite
the one taken by the real aggressor.

Imitating the ritual performance
of two male cats competing for a female,
both fish stalk each other angrily
to get the weak fish to back down.
Neither fish gives in.
Did Sybil ever submit to herself—
thus having one personality fight another and win?
What would Freud say
if a human displayed such bizarre behavior?

Helpless, just like the Betta,
is nature in the hands of man.
Our earth has been continually tortured
by wars and substances which poison our atmosphere.
Man is an ever-present mirror.
When will we lay down our weapons
and stop annihilating ourselves?

October 1988

Severed Heart

A severed friendship with a wounded heart
eventually heals—
through tears it heals.

Hurt can be erased from the slate of one's soul.
Forgiveness through love is the most powerful cleanser.

Intimacy can't be killed.
It can only be faded
just as the memory
of an acquaintance
soon disappears.

Slowly this fading process has begun.
Both parties are now free
to wander on new roads
and explore different paths.

The past should never be blackened.
Something beautiful does not need to be made ugly.
Nor does a beautiful memory
become ugly on its own.

A forward stride
is sufficient
to refresh the eye.

Just as gentle showers after a storm are welcomed,
so shall rain be cherished
by mending hearts.

October 18, 1988

Synergy

I will follow you where you need to go.
Follow me when I need to lead.
Hold my hand forever and we won't get lost.

When one of us veers to the left or to the right,
let's trade perspectives and see what it is that the other sees.
It is easier to read a map when another steers.
If one of us is always watching, we won't miss the falling star.

I will lend you my dreams when your vision is blurred
and your spirit has fled.
I will lend you my rainbow when your world does not have color
and you have grown tired of a black and white screen.
May I borrow your strength when the load I carry
pulls us both off our paths?
Will you renew my hunger when I no longer strive?

Let's clear a new trail in our favorite woods.
Let's taste again the flavor of cookies made from scratch.
Every step brings us closer to hidden treasure.
If we believe that everything that glitters is gold,
we will never be broke.

Sketch a picture while I write the rough draft of a poem.
When we have both finished,
we can see if your picture illustrates my words
and if my words add meaning to your picture.

It is easier to build a house from a floor plan than from a vision.
Let's make one collage together
and race towards its image
with the vigor of a child in a toy store.
Help me glue each piece carefully as a cat would groom each hair.
If we build our house together, we can build a strong foundation.
If we join our candles together, we will never have to walk in the dark.
You are my artist and I love you.

January 21, 1992

Vile Love

Ocean waves, please soothe all anger.
Lay to rest the embittered heart.
Annoyed by petty complaints,
vengeance hisses like a snake before an attack.
It pleads from the depth of its being.
No one stands a chance against its vile love.
More potent than poison,
the tongue always demands retaliation.

Retreat swiftly to your guitar.
The stringed doctor is your medicine.
As a surgeon disinfects a wound before removing a bullet,
create another sad song to cleanse your pain.

Young one, never surrender your hope.
Do not fade into the land of lost melodies
where retrieval may not happen.
A falling star does not disintegrate
until it gives birth to a dream.

Perseverance is a glistening constant.
A mask of resentment will not permanently disfigure the soul.
Anger will dissipate unless it is fed.

Although love remains undefined,
its expressions approach infinity.
Absolute comprehension is inconceivable.
Love prevails only when it is both understood and welcomed.

May 18, 1992

Nighttime

Night drifts in and silence takes over.

Nothing moves.

No one thinks.

All emotion has been erased.

Only emptiness remains.

Void

Void

Existence has passed into oblivion.

Serenity has permeated the very being of life itself.

Every breath has been snuffed out.

Reality is now a memory

with no one left to remember it.

May 19, 1992

The Face

The face is a legacy of every person,
that some can't forget.
The memory of every man, woman, and child
is implanted in their minds forever.

Each time a face is encountered,
the process of recognition begins—
déjà vu exploration,
past reconciliation,
the hazy bonding of two facades.

Although the image may be displaced—
Its very profile erased,
the impression has been encased,
inside the vault where input is embraced.

Although man might not comprehend
the encoding process in its entirety,
the beauty of a face remains.

There is strength in its familiarity.
It is the foci of most portraits—
the glamorous form by which we are known.

A face represents the soul.
Those who can't forget a face
often fail to understand
how others can fail
to recognize a soul.

Alas, a stroke maims the spirit
and castrates the mind.

It can damage the communication
between the two hemispheres of a brain
and interfere with the recognition
of a face.

October 31, 1992

Vain Vows

"I love you,"
said the woman to her son
as she spanked him and hugged him
and threatened him with a gun.

"I'll wait for you,"
said a woman to her man
as he headed off to war
to rid the enemy from the land.

But her vow was never kept
though the fighting had just begun.
Their lips had barely parted
when, by another, her heart had been won.

"Goodbye Dad. I'll visit you,"
said the man to his father
but no one recognized him
when all the mourners gathered.

The son never knew his father's date of birth,
so only his name and date of death were inscribed.
"I love you" he never said.
The right moment had not arrived.

"I will serve you,"
said the man to the Lord.
"To you I make this promise, that I will preach your word."

Although many prayers were offered,
no sermon was ever spoken.
His will remained his own
and his Bible was seldom opened.

Tomorrow never comes
when promises are made in vain.

October 7, 1993

The Pier

Alone on a pier,
I wait for the sun to rise.

A solitary leaf,
gracefully drops into the water.

Slowly, it begins
its long journey
to the other side.

Nestled underneath
grandmother's old quilt blanket,
I am protected
from the chilling wind
but not from sleep's powerful grasp.

Surrounded
by the chatter of birds,
I watch them play hide-in-go-seek
as they try to escape
my watchful eye.

A chorus
of distinctive voices
blends into a well-rehearsed symphony
and lulls me
quickly into the land of dreams.

October 31, 1993

Symphony of Waves

Crisp emerald waves
smash against the slippery rocks.
Their rhythmic patterns massage
the awaiting stones.

Instantly transformed into white foam,
nature's bubble-bath
generously sprinkles its cold mist.

Scattered strands of tangled algae
lurk beneath the ocean's crest.
Moss creeps across the retaining walls
like a prowler staking out its territory.

Reminiscent of the Chicago River
on Saint Patrick's Day,
the sunlight paints
its sea green reflection on the enchanted canvas.

A crashing tumble,
followed by a great applause,
sounds like simmering bacon,
splattering in grease.

The echoes of the sailors' lullaby
are quickly extinguished
when exiting from the symphony of waves.

1994

Lost Chances

Hateful spirit
Feeds on power
Gifts that woo and steal innocence
The sacrifice yet to come

Flesh for freedom
Pleasure for peace
The price of love

Wasted dreams and shattered lives
Erased memories shield the hidden pain.
The broken child grieves alone.

Damaged, afraid, and without hope,
one by one, the little children surrender.

A generation of victims await their chance.

Who will tell the children that there are no more chances?

1994

Time

Catch it.
Hold it.
Stop it.
Control it.
Make it go faster,
and then slower.
Backward
And then forward
Make it last as long as you want and,
end when you want.

Erase it or relive it.
Trade it or forget it.
Give it away or let it slip away.
Revolt against its power and,
then, admonish it for its beauty.
Hunger after it.

Such a priceless commodity
The envy of all who have wasted it
Their wanton look
When they have depleted their final share

Consume it,
before it consumes you.

January 14, 1994

Soar On Wings Like Eagles

A pauper trudges alone across the city streets.
He drags with him a broken wheelbarrow
filled with junk.
Mismatched tools, rags, and broken glassware
impart security by stealing freedom.

Having accomplished the tasks of kings,
the dutiful and humble servant
awaits with patience the bestowing of honors.
The moment of recognition never arrives.

The fearless warrior returns from battle
and announces his presence with shouts of victory,
"We have won! Our enemies are dead!"
The villagers do not hear him because they too are dead.

O great warrior, what prize can you claim
that could bring back the dead?
Even your trusted horse has been sacrificed.
What have you won?

Where does the eagle fly
when it soars with great majesty
towards its secret destination?

With the superior grace of a ballerina
and the skill of an expert pilot,
the majestic bird glides purposefully
across God's stage.

Its wings flutter freely.
Its claws have released all prey
and all that binds him to earth.
Gradually, it disappears into the twilight.

When I was a child, my mother said I could fly.
I believed her though I didn't have wings.
She told me that if I was happy,
I would have wings in my dreams and
those wings could take me anywhere.

I have flown with that eagle on many journeys.
I have fed that man and sold his baggage.
He now has a bed and a roof over his head.
I have thanked that servant many times.
I even helped the warrior build a new village
and locate a lost brother.

When I was no longer a child
I stopped dreaming I had wings.
Although I wanted to dream of flying again,
flights of soaring became only a memory.

I have often wished that I had flown to more places
before the dreams stopped.
Without my wings,
I am confined to earth
where I will fade into the nothingness
of oblivion.

January 24, 1994

A Few of My Favorite Things

Family portraits in matching frames
Fancy fish with vibrant colors
Funny squawks by beluga whales
Finding seashells
Flashes of sunlight following rain
Fading rainbows
Fall leaves
Floating freely on a lake
First publication
Freedom to speak, to write, and to be heard
Faith that protects
Fresh cut flowers with a note
Fireside chats
Foamy suds in a bath
Frosty mug with root beer
Fits of laughter
Forever friends
Futon, bolster, pillow, and quilt
Felt pen and paper
Fairy tale or fable book
Fruit and almond tea
Fragrance of vanilla candles
Feline friend with furry kisses
Finished races
Fish sizzling on an outdoor grill
Festivals and plays
Flame-like hues of sunrise and sunset
Flying in my dreams

November 6, 1994

Ode to the Lighthouse

Guide our craft gently through all raging storms.
Shine forth your light and lead her home.

Your presence is a rock
that crushes the fear of being lost at sea.
Like the Great Protector,
may the radiance of your beacon's light
never fail.

The tower is our guardian angel
that welcomes our vessel back to shore.

Good captain, may life's storms
never be so great that you lose hope
and abandon ship.

Dear shipmates, pray that your captain
does not lose his way
and stray off course.

At sunset
after your final voyage,
when the seas are calm,
may the Great Protector guide you home.

February 22, 1995

Imprisoned Emotions—The Final Plague

DISAPPOINTMENT
Pleasure that is tasted for a moment
and then ripped away

REGRET
Demons that destroy joy
by re-opening wounds
of failures and moments of indecision

SOLITUDE
Prayer closets
where demons of regret are slain

DOUBT
Fear that the road not taken
was in fact greener

LIES
Belief that man is innately good
and tomorrow is infinite

LOVE
Not being afraid
to relinquish the reins
of one's emotions to another

Emotions are the true reflections of one's humanity,
revealed in silence,
through the written word.

August 26, 1995

In Pursuit of Naught

Words spew forth
without fear of repercussion
without fear at all.
No holds barred
under the reign
of a venting tongue

Leaves launch forth
in their annual journey.
One glorious leap
in pursuit of freedom

They aim
for the vast dull canvas
where they present
their perfect coat
of many colors
to the barren trees.

Time wanders
as it waits.
Time watches
as it appears to linger.
Time elapses suddenly
with the waning
of a final tock.

And then there was silence,
with no applause

September 20, 1995

The Tree

I saw a tree today.

It was the biggest Sycamore in Connecticut.

I wanted to climb it,

but I didn't have the right shoes on.

Last week I had the right shoes on,

but I didn't have the time.

Next week I will pass this way again

and I don't think I will climb it then either.

Perhaps, it will be because I will be too tired.

When I am old

and many years have passed,

will the tree still be there to climb?

I think I will be too old to climb it then.

March 1, 1996

Destination—Freedom

An instinctive drive to survive
propels this creature onward
with full force.

The motivation behind
its purposeful effort is unclear.

Perhaps,
it is driven
by hunger
or perhaps, it moves
to satisfy a thirst.

I like to think
it moves in pursuit
of a greater need—freedom.

If only man's ambition
could be as focused
as the innate initiative of this turtle.

August 31, 1996

Dreams

Despite our best efforts,
too often,
completion of all our life's endeavors
escapes us.

Though we carefully try to plan each detail
to avoid making mistakes,
the time and energy we expend
is spent in vain.

Magnificent charm
is found in imperfection.

Many pass into eternity
without having had the chance
to check their rainbow
for its infamous pot of gold.

Though our rainbows are unique
and our pots of gold differ,
the extent we esteem them
is the same.

We look to them
for inspiration and purpose
as we strive to achieve,
the tasks we want to accomplish.

Often, we live out our entire lives
in pursuit of fool's gold.

When will we learn
to look for rainbows in the right places?

September 1, 1996

Journey to the Land of the Purple Flowers

I see fields of purple flowers in the distance
and I want to run through them,
but they are too far away.

Despite my best efforts to reach their sanctuary,
they remain just beyond my grasp.

I imagine their aroma surrounding me
while I dance in the wind
dressed in lavender garb.

While I dance,
I am accompanied by
a sprightly melody
performed by an obscured source
within the flowers.

When I stop dancing
to identify the lyrics,
the sound abruptly ceases.
If I approach the flowers to identify the singer,
the flowers disappear.
It's as if they don't want
their magic discovered.

Within the presence of their silent splendor,
no questions are ever asked
because answers are not needed.

The flowers are a memorial to simpler times
when worries were insignificant
and harmony reigned.

I come here to gaze at the flowers
to renew my hope
in the existence of peace.

Legend has it,
that a great forest lies behind the flowers.
Somewhere, within that forest,
is a door to another land.

The key to that door has been hidden
amongst the flowers.
To find it, would mean,
many flowers would be trampled,
and their beauty spoiled.

Sojourners came here,
intending to search for the key.
But they soon departed,
without stepping on a single flower.

Before I leave,
I memorize their image.
I always return before the image fades.
I fear that if the image fades,
my dreams will fade.

The land of the purple flowers
is a place where children frolic
and everyone is a child.

September 20, 1996

Tomorrow

How many faces have been forgotten?
How many friendships have slipped away?
How much time has passed?
How many people have passed?

How many stories have not been shared?
How many letters have not been sent?
How many questions have never been asked?
How many answers have never been given?

How much in life have we forgotten?

Too often, we wait for perfection
before we share our talents.
Too often, perfection never comes
and the chance is lost.

November 30, 1996

Inspiration

One petal,
can inspire the creation of art.

One glance at a work of art,
can inspire the search for beauty.

One search for beauty,
can inspire the viewing of a sunset.

One beautiful sunset,
can inspire a poet.

One poet,
can inspire the right to dream.

One person who dreams,
can inspire many to dream.

January 9, 1997

Soul Hugs

A hug so complete
that there's no separation
between two souls, two hearts,
and the spirit that unites them

A vacant heart
is an anchor to forward motion.
A soul hug
replenishes nothingness
and reveals the anchor's impermanence.

A soul hug
does not conduct
an inventory of errors
to blame the impetus of failure.
It does not demand dialogue
and an analysis of events
to teach a lesson.
It provides comfort, compassion,
and understanding
to release the weight.

Dreams stacked like JENGA blocks
teeter on top of missing pieces
that collapse and scatter.
A soul hug
conquers anguish
and disentangles the web
that tethers dreams.

Restoration of moxie commences
once decimation of volition ceases.
After evil chokes
and snuffs out hope,
a soul hug
restores fortitude,
creates light,
and ignites the belief
that one can fly again.

January 21, 2020

What the Fox Squirrel Didn't Say

I saw you.
You saw me.
I watched you.
You watched me.
I admired your genius
for a quarter of an hour.
Mesmerized by your
exquisite visage,
I returned to my home
to retrieve my phone.
I wanted to capture a photo
to preserve this memory.
You waited for me,
as if you understood,
that I was a witness
to your existence.

I contemplated the possibility
that you presented yourself
as an appeal for help.
Like the *Lorax* (Dr. Seuss, 1971),
who spoke for the trees
because they lacked tongues,
perhaps, you needed a voice
to alert the construction workers
that your family lived there.
Like the *Who*,
in Horton Hears a Who (Dr. Seuss, 1982),
all the fox squirrels needed to shout in unison,
"We are here! We are here! We are here! We are here!"

Hammers, saws,
and earsplitting machinery—
a cacophony of marauders
plunder the forest.
As blasts shatter the melody of the woods,
you remain lionhearted and unshakable,
yet bewildered.
There is irony in construction—
a home can be simultaneously built
while another home is destroyed.

Like the *Lorax*, I am "shortish" and "oldish"
and I have a voice
that is "sharpish" and "bossy." (Dr. Seuss, 1971.)
I want to always be willing to be a voice
on behalf of those whose voices are not heard.

I wish I had the authority
to tell these workers,
"Stop cutting down the trees!"

I wish I could tell all people,
"Stop wasting the resources
that we have been given—
family, friendship, community,
education, language, words,
faith, and prayer."

Five months after our fairytale-like encounter,
you still haven't approached me again,
though I searched for you.

I believe you understood,
that I had genuine intentions
to only show you kindness.
But I couldn't promise,
that all other humans would be kind too.

May you remain
curious and confident,
gentle and patient,
a silent communicator,
a courageous ambassador of family,
and a protector of trees.

Thank you for entrusting your message
to a human.

April 25, 2020

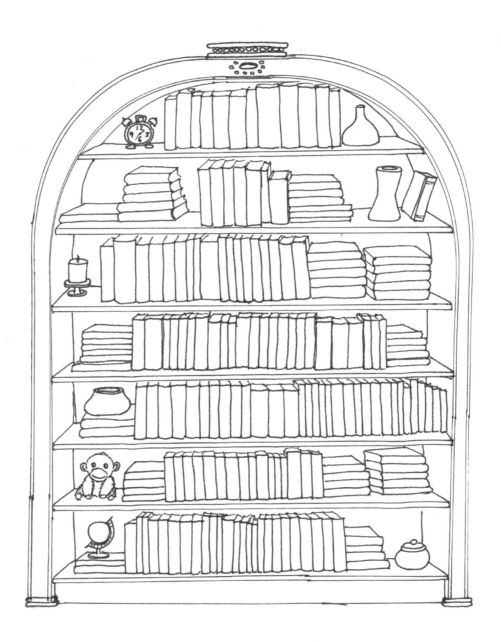

The Collection

Capture
Camouflage
Conceal
Obscure
Overcriticize
Omit
Reflect
Regret
Rekindle
Occupy
Organize
Own
Notice
Neutralize
Numb
Awaken
Amass
Arrest

Imagine
Illustrate
Interpret
Save
Scrutinize
Scatter

Believe
Blame
Bury
Agitate
Alter
Analyze
Describe
Display
Destroy

This is what I do with my memories.

Heal
Hold
Hope
Educate
Effect
Exemplify
Accept
Advise
Assimilate
Learn
Lose
Love
Impact
Inspire
Instruct
Nurture
Navigate
Narrate
Guard
Grow
Give

Protect
Process
Publish
Reconstruct
Reminisce
Release
Adapt
Amuse
Appreciate
Yarn
Yearn
Yield
Emancipate
Empower
Enjoy
Rebuild
Release
Remember
Seize
Savor
Share

Storytelling
Symbolize
Scribe
Erase
Explore
Express
Need
Normalize
Novelize
Taste
Transform
Treasure

This is what I want to do with my memories.

May 29, 2020

Imperfect

A muzzle inhibits my bite
and squelches my voice.
There is a bit in my mouth
attached to taut and unyielding reins.

I am anatomically dressed in paunch and full-bodied attire
that I didn't choose to wear.
I am cloaked with envy of women with svelte figures
in size two clothing.

I drive past a committee of turkey vultures
engaged in a debate about which carcass to devour next.
How is it that a vulture can choose what to eat, when to eat, and where to eat
but a resident of a nursing home cannot?
They resemble a clip of the political committee meeting
that aired during the morning news.
I watch the exquisite flight of a kettle of these birds approach heaven
and I regret making this comparison.

Shredded parmesan cheese strands
submerge garlic croutons in lobster bisque.
I ingest one succulent bite after another
aiding my Bohemian soup spoon as it masquerades as a lifeboat.
I am an accomplice as it transports the croutons to the good ship, *Down the Hatch*.
Whom has not been beguiled by an imposter lifeboat?

I realize that I have incessantly relinquished the reins that control my life.
During a myriad of infinitesimal moments,
I have empowered others to reign at my helm.

"…when you were younger you dressed yourself and went where you wanted; but when you are old you
will stretch out your hands, and someone else will dress you and lead you where you do not want to
go." (John 21:18, New International Version.)

I didn't stop this from happening to my mother
and, one day, I fear, my daughter won't stop this from happening to me.

My attempt to grasp hold of the reins and re-claim them are futile.
They morph into sand and instantly vanish in my hands.
They were only a hologram; perhaps they never actually existed.

February 5, 2021

Mom

I wanted to write you a love letter before you died,
to make sure you knew how much you meant to me,
before your soul left earth for heaven.

A day or two before my final Zoom call with you,
I felt an inner nudging prompting me that it was time
to write you a final letter,
but I didn't write it.
I didn't want to listen to the urgency in my spirit
warning me it was time for you to leave.
I pretended not to hear it,
hoping that you could stay longer.

A barrage of unwritten words and feelings invaded my heart.
I blocked them in and refused to release them.
I didn't give my tears permission to fall either,
but they couldn't be contained in a broken heart.

The first time I gave you an orchid,
you wrote a letter to thank me.
You told me that you had always wanted one
but that you thought it cost too much
for someone to buy it for you.
I wish you knew that to me,
you were worth an infinite number of orchids.

Orchids remind me of your tenacity to bloom
despite adversity
even in places where virtue is deliberately strangled.

I cried when a stroke made you forget how to make coffee.
Although strokes stole your memory
and the COVID-19 pandemic robbed you of human touch,
neither erased the salt and light in your soul.
At times I viewed the destruction of your memory as a gift.
You forgot what made you cry.
For twenty years I tried to replace your negative memories
with twice as many positive ones.

When I was a child, you woke me up each morning
with the tune of a Fisher Price clock.
You or I have kept this clock for more than fifty years.

During the Christmas when I gave it back to you as a present,
you revered it as if you had been re-united with a dear friend.
At times the clock made you sad
because it reminded you how quickly time passes.

When you were in a nursing home,
you once broke your hip
trying to prevent your roommate from tripping
over the call wires attached to her bed.
On another occasion you fell
while trying to wash the windows,
to make your view of the birds more vivid.

You never lost your compassion
for those who were less fortunate.
You were oblivious to the fact
that you had less than them.
During times when I had plenty,
I tried to share what I had with you.
It sometimes frustrated me that you would give away
much of what I gave you.

You remained sassy, stubborn, and feisty
until a few months before you died.
I once watched you drag your IV cart to the nurses' station
to demand that they give you salt.
I admired your grit as you presented your case.
You have outsmarted each of your children
when we tried to retrieve a saltshaker from your hand.

I am thankful you planted within me
a strength of faith
that will nourish me all my life.

I love you.

March 29, 2021

Apprehending Thieves of Lost Words

I awake inspired by a dozen jumbled ideas.
They take my pneuma hostage
and demand their inklings be composed.
I resist.
Instead, I riffle through social media
in search of faux droll entertainment.
Nothing captures my interest.
So, I resume sleep.

When I reawake,
I realize that thieves, in retaliation for my refusal to write,
have stolen my ideas.
They temporarily relocated them to my hippocampus
where they will be erased
unless I negotiate with my prefrontal neurons.
Their demands?
Immortality—they are vying for space in a poem.

A bird trills during my morning walk.
I attempt to locate the source.
I find him cloaked by leaves but still warbling
He is miffed that I have discovered his hiding place
and interrupted his solo.
He halts his performance, frowns his beak,
and retreats away from pesky humans.

I return home to make soup.
I simmer vegetables and herbs from my garden.
Then, in pursuit of epicurean perfection, I add spice.
The finale commences when I cajole a taster.
My fulfillment is in creation not consumption.

At dawn the next day,
I attempt to record
the collision of a kaleidoscope with a symphony.
The music of the ocean and the hues of the sky
become my muse.
The moment when the sun
greets the waves in a kiss
is photographic perfection.

I laughed when Juno,
a beluga whale at the Mystic Aquarium in CT,
opened his mouth wide to startle little children.
I smiled when he spat water
over the tank wall
that landed on top of his audience.
But I celebrated freedom from captivity
watching belugas,
the canaries of the sea,
leap like ballerinas
in the open water of Tadoussac in Quebec, Canada.

I linger in a tub or jacuzzi as if time were infinite.
I recline amongst the sandpipers,
watching them scurry,
as if they were late for an important meeting.
I no longer scurry.

Huddled under my grandmother's quilt,
my family snacks on ribs and dumplings
while watching Nancy Drew.
I wonder how television would portray her
assisting with the apprehension of the thieves
of my lost words?

April 18, 2021

Hairline Fractures in the Heart

One thousand tears
from one thousand cuts
unseen and unspoken
does not mean
non-existent.

Cracks weaken foundations.
A void festers into a sinkhole.
Microscopic now
Atomic later
Salty tears dissolve diamonds.

One drop of blood
in an ocean
isn't noticed,
until it attracts a shark
with a fatal bite.

Eyes that don't see beauty
Ears that refuse to hear
A mouth that does not kiss
Arms that forget to caress
A heart that withholds love

One thousand tears
from one thousand cuts
unseen and unspoken
does not mean
non-existent.

September 14, 2021

Dry Bones Come Alive

I take him out of the closet so I can dance with him.
I am careful to only choose my beloved skeleton.
The other skeletons can't move
unless specifically chosen by someone,
who wants a particular one to dance again.
Unless that happens, it will remain as dry bones in the closet.

I grasp the fingers of a bony hand
of the one I love
with my flesh-covered hand.
I place my arms around the lifeless essence in front of me
and I lead it to where moonlight surrounds it.
I allow my heart to penetrate the vacant cavity
where its heart used to be
and I listen to the silence while I wait.
Then, I offer my heart.
His absent heart can only return
if I first offer my heart.
And even after I have offered it,
until we dance,
I won't know if his heart will beat again
in unison with mine.

One conjoined breath reawakens our song
just as it did when the music first roused us.
The ties to these bones remain immortal and unbroken—
more enduring than ligaments that attach bone to bone.
When dry bones become alive and step again,
their core is refreshed with potentiality and jubilation
of soul and spirit.
They dance with more rhythm and vigor
than those with bones encased in flesh that never died.
The warmth of skin returns.
Tendons reattach.
The rattling of bones vanishes.
Moonlight shadows reveal the bliss and fervor of our ecstasy.
An exuberant breeze lifts our feet,
and we spin and gallop with the pizazz of all our being.

When the maker of the wind breathes life into dry bones,
bygone skeletons eagerly frolic and dance again.

November 10, 2021

Shadow Dance (Valedictory)

Shine where you shine.
Walk on your chosen path.
You will shine if you are on that path.
It is where purpose meets heart.

An explanation is not required
about why you have chosen this path
except to those closest to you.
They should know the impetus
of why you walk where you do.

Offer what you have to offer.
Don't offer what you don't have.
If you don't have extra energy,
don't offer to complete extra tasks.

Be whom you want to be
and not whom others want you to be.

You might decide to change,
as you learn and grow.
Whether or not you choose to change,
is up to you.
Leave behind
those who don't embrace your changes.

Strive to become your best self—
a better person tomorrow than today.
And when you have days this doesn't happen,
try again tomorrow.

Only look back to reminisce about cherished moments
or to learn from mistakes.
Don't allow past failures
to dim your future luminosity.

Surround yourself with those who see your luster.
During times when you can't shine,
dance in the shadow
of the light of a friend.
Be the kind of friend
who allows others
to dance in the shadow of your light.

January 22, 2022

Jacob

When siblings,
mothers, fathers, spouses,
or "friends"
continue to evoke tears,
think of the name *Jacob*.

Jacob means supplanter.
Synonyms of supplanter include:
Substitute
Replacement
Relief
Surrogate
Proxy
Equivalent
Alternative
Backup
Delegate
Successor
Stand-in
Fill in

When loved ones
fail to love,
fail to protect,
or intentionally destroy,
their connections
will be unbound,
broken,
and erased.

Jacob will take their place.
Recognize,
welcome,
and embrace *Jacob*.
Wait for *Jacob*.

April 3, 2022

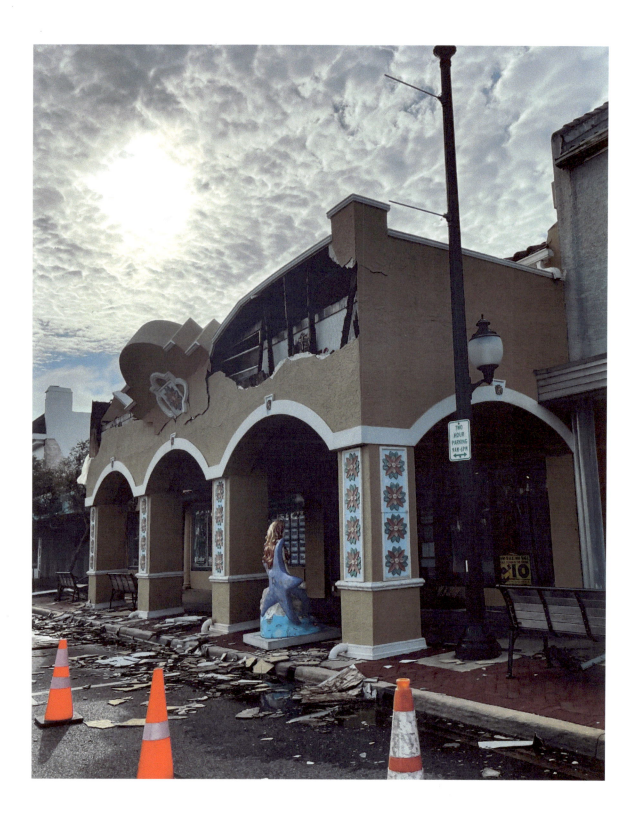

Hurricane Ian

(Before There Was a Storm…)

Waiting for the sprinkling of Pixie Dust
to enable flight

Wishing for an awakening of fireflies
to sparkle the night

Watching for moments of emotion
to stir me to write

Dancing and singing in the pool
under the moonlight

(The Storm…)

Packing clothes, water, and food
so we could survive

Filling both of our gas tanks
so we could just drive

Shielding plants and flowers
so they stay alive

Playing games using flashlights,
we remain inside.

Waiting for landfall
of Ian's destructive path

Watching scary weather news
from my bubble bath

Listening in the dark
for the wind to calm its wrath

Hoping our roof will stay intact
in the aftermath

(After the Storm…)

Palm trees scattered like dominoes.
Buildings crumbled too.

Street signs, stop signs, and lamp posts
were all blown askew.

Cars and debris floated on streets;
storm surge rage was cruel.

Islands and coasts became ghost towns.
The death toll list grew.

Replacing a broken roof vent
Throwing out the food

Buying all six loaves of bread,
man in store was rude.

Four stores and still no milk
Fearing gas line feud

No power; no internet; no school
Mood was subdued.

October 2022

The Last Plight

It's called the last plight—
the journey to the light—
the final attempt to make it right.

It's the last song
the last dance
the last poem
the last chance.

It's the last good-bye
before someone dies.

It's the final walk
to the other side.

It's too late
to put out fires
on bridges
that have already been burned.

It's too late
to mend a bridge
when the bridge
or the person crossing it
is no longer present.

When the music stops
it's too late to dance.

December 31, 1996

Life

Unwritten novels
Undeveloped film
Shadows on the wall
play in the night.
Only little children watch them play.

Lightly drawn lines
Shallow roots
Raise the anchor
to sail away.

Awake early
to witness the path
of the rising sun.
Watch for the day
when the sun is darkened.

Lost time
Neglected dreams
Guilty for eternity
Selfish desires
Plenty that is never shared
Fulfillment is a mist to those who seek it.

A poet doesn't die
until the last poem is written.
Even the poet does not know which poem will be the last,
until the author drifts forever,
in the land of dreams.

Write until sleep overtakes the spirit.
Write until dreams overtake reality.
Write until the last poem is finished.
Write until the pen falls to the floor.
Write until the last poet has fallen.

April 8, 1995

Disclaimer

Although I have included dates when I originally wrote each poem, I have found that my poetry is at times fluid and, as a result, I have modified some words or punctuation in some poems. I didn't keep track of which poems I changed. The dates remain the original dates when each poem was first created, even if the poem included some modifications. My poems are works in progress just as each person is a work in progress.

ABOUT THE AUTHOR:

I am married and have one daughter. I have been writing poetry since childhood. I have worked in foster-care agencies, schools, and as a private consultant for three and a half decades. As an active BCBA certificant, I have provided ABA services to military families with children with ASDs. My husband and I were specialized foster-care providers/CTH providers for twenty years. In addition to writing, I enjoy kayaking, photography, and traveling. I own Action Behavioral Consulting LLC which owns Koa Books and Stationery. My email address is: koabooksandstationery@gmail.com

ABOUT THE ARTISTS:

Tricia Robinson Harvey is married and has one son. She resides in South Carolina. She has been an artist by trade since 1989. She owns Tricia Harvey Designs which has its own Facebook page. Tricia specializes in murals and uses many mediums in her art. She is a member of Dreamline Artists.

She completed ten illustrations that have been included in *Flying in My Dreams*.

This is her second illustration project for a book.

Alexander Chen is a freelance artist from Alpharetta, Georgia. His artwork explores nature and wildlife, with a focus on realism and bold colors. Alexander's other creative interests include reading, writing, and cooking. (His mother was the first peer I became friends with on the first day of kindergarten.)

Karen A. Johnson produces art for her business, Karen's Nature Art. It is art inspired by nature—reflections of God's glory. She has Bachelors' degrees in biological illustration and entomology, the study of insects. Karen is a member of the Guild of National Science Illustrators (GNSI) and the Nature Artist Guild of the Morton Arboretum where she regularly exhibits her work. Karen does most of her color work in watercolor, gouache, acrylic and pastel and her black and white work on scratchboard. Her website is: www.karensnatureart.com

Kai Sprunger is a Junior in high school, and she lives with her parents—Rene and Ange Sprunger. In her free time, she enjoys creating digital art as well as pursuing art in other forms such as origami and jewelry-making. Her artwork is inspired by the sky and by surrealism.

Rene Sprunger is the author's husband. He has a degree in Electrical Engineering. In his leisure time he enjoys drawing and spending time with the family. He welcomes the opportunity to make two illustrations for his wife's book and to assist her with technical aspects of the publication process.

CPSIA information can be obtained
at www.ICGtesting.com
Printed in the USA
LVHW072027060523
746150LV00003B/11